The Road To Modern Music

PAUL EMERICH

17461

© Copyright 1960 by SOUTHERN MUSIC PUBLISHING COMPANY, INC.
International Copyright Secured   Printed in U. S. A.
All Rights Reserved Including the Right of Public Performance for Profit

"WARNING! Any person who copies or arranges all or part of the words or music of this musical composition shall be liable to an action for injunction, damages and profits under the United States Copyright Law."

SOUTHERN MUSIC PUBLISHING COMPANY, INC.   NEW YORK

MT
40
E534
1960

PREFACE

These basic studies of applied modern music consist of scales in unconventional combinations, passages in non-traditional sequences, harmonic and melodic patterns as employed by modern composers, which have not been dealt with previously in exercises of the piano literature.

Through these studies, designed to stimulate the imagination of the musician with new patterns of melodic and harmonic progressions, the conventionally trained ear should become acquainted with the unconventional characteristics of contemporary music. They train him to become more intimately familiar with the world of dissonances toward which he might have had, until now, a negative attitude.

This work aims to fill the gap with which all are confronted who approach modern music, due to the lack of studies or any other kind of appropriate exercises anticipating the new technical problems. Etudes and model-exercises exist only to prepare the pianist for traditional music. All studies, whether by Czerny, Chopin, Moszkowski or Rachmaninoff, are composed in the conventional vein, with traditional harmonies and progressions. The few etudes written by Scriabin, Stravinsky, Bartók and other modern composers may be called etudes only by virtue of their character, but they do not serve as practicing material for students of modern music.

Music composed in the Twelve-Tone system, with its sheer limitless tone-permutations, can not be forced into any scheme since the principle of repetition is not applicable.

This presentation of new musical and pianistic ideas will serve as a helpful guide for performers and composers alike, aiding pianists in preparation for arising technical problems and attracting music lovers to the unfamiliar music of our time.

I should like to express my gratitude to my wife Rose and to my friend and student Rudolf Schaar for their invaluable help in preparing the manuscript, and to Southern Music Publishing Company, Inc. for their early envisioning of the vital need for this work.

Paul Emerich

TABLE OF CONTENTS

(According to chronological development)

IA	The Two Whole-tone Scales	3
IB	Augmented Triads, Seventh Chords and other Combinations within the Whole-tone Scales	4
II	The Modes Applied in Modern Music	6
IIIA	The Pentatonic Scales	7
IIIB	Black and White Keys in Contrast	8
IIIC	The Sixte ajoutee	10
IVA	Bitonal Combinations of Major and Minor Scales	11
IVB	Bitonal and Polytonal Combinations of Triads and other Chords	12
VA	Bitonal Combinations of the Two Whole-tone Scales	15
VB	Bitonal Combinations of Major, Minor and Augmented Triads, as well as other Chords within the Whole-tone Scales	15
VIA	Dislocations of Traditional Harmonic Relations, "Twisted Cadences" and other Alterations	17
VIB	Polytonality through passages and "Telescoping" Harmonies (*zusammengeschoben*)	18
VIIA	Expansions and Contractions of the Traditional Scales	19
VIIB	Expansions and Contractions of Intervals: Thirds, Sixths, and as Diminished Octaves, the Sevenths	20
VIIC	Expansions and Contractions of Harmonic Structures	22
VIID	Expansions and Contractions: Melody Deviations (*Irregular Progressions*)	24
VIIIA	Chords and Progressions of Fourths and Fifths	25
VIIIB	Chords and Progressions of Seconds and Ninths (*Augmented Octaves*)	27
VIIIC	Tone-clusters	29
IX	Polyrhythm and Crossrhythm	31
X	Twelve-tone Music	32
	Index of Composers	33

ABBREVIATIONS

AME--American Music Edition
AMP--Associated Music Publishers Inc.
B & H--Boosey & Hawkes Inc. (Ltd.)
C.F.--Carl Fischer, Inc.
Dd--Durand & Cie
EAM--Editorial Argentina de Musica
ECIC--Editorial Cooperativa Interamericana de Compositores
Elk.--Elkin & Co.
Esch.--Max Eschig
Fr.--E. Fromont
IMC--International Music Company
NM--New Music
Schr.--G. Schirmer, Inc.
SMPC--Southern Music Publishing Company, Inc.
U.E.--Universal Edition

l.: line, m.: measure, mvt: movement, p.: page

Explanation of signs:

$L^{\varnothing}$ Left hand one octave lower

//   to be continued in the same manner

IA
The Two Whole-tone Scales

© Copyright 1960 by SOUTHERN MUSIC PUBLISHING COMPANY, INC.
International Copyright Secured
Printed in U.S.A.
All Rights Reserved Including the Right of Public Performance for Profit

Claude Debussy - JARDINS SOUS LA PLUIE, p. 20 l. 3 & 4
Used by permission of Durand & Cie., Paris, Copyright Owners
Elkan-Vogel Co., Inc., Phila., Pa., Sole Agents

Béla Bartók - SUITE op. 14, p. 5 l. 4 m. 2-5
Copyright 1918 by Universal Edition (London) Ltd. Renewed 1945
Copyright and Renewal assigned to Boosey & Hawkes Inc. for U.S.A.
Used by permission of Universal Edition (London) Ltd. and Boosey & Hawkes Inc.

R. G. Morillo - CONJUROS, p. 3 l. 4 m. 2-4, l. 5, l. 6 m. 1, p. 10 l. 4-5, p. 11 l. 1
Used by permission of Editorial Cooperativa Interamericana de Compositores, Montevideo
Sole Representatives: Southern Music Publishing Company, Inc., New York

FOR REFERENCE:

Debussy - CHILDREN'S CORNER, IV "The Snow is Dancing", Dd, p. 17 l. 4
VOILES, Dd
Bartók - MIKROKOSMOS, B & H, Vol. 5, p. 32, p. 33, p. 34
Rebikoff - LES DEMONS S'AMUSENT, Schr. (album)

IB

Augmented Triads, Seventh Chords and other Combinations within the Whole-tone Scales

Combination of the two triads within a whole-tone scale (telescoping)

sempre con Ped.

Ex. 1 — Claude Debussy - REFLETS DANS L'EAU, p. 4 l. 4 & 5
Used by permission of Durand & Cie., Paris, Copyright Owners
Elkan-Vogel Co., Inc., Phila., Pa., Sole Agents

Ex. 2 — Maurice Ravel - JEUX D'EAU, p. 1 l. 2 m. 2, l. 3
Used by permission of B. F. Wood Music Company

Ex. 3 — Charles T. Griffes - THE WHITE PEACOCK, p. 1 l. 1 & 2
Copyright 1917 by G. Schirmer, Inc., International Copyright Secured
Copyright Renewal assigned, 1945, to G. Schirmer, Inc.
Used by permission of G. Schirmer, Inc.

Ex. 4 — Béla Bartók - SUITE op. 14, p. 6 l. 1-4
Copyright 1918 by Universal Edition (London) Ltd., Renewed 1945
Copyright and Renewal assigned to Boosey & Hawkes Inc. for U.S.A.
Used by permission of Universal Edition (London) Ltd., and Boosey & Hawkes Inc.

Ex. 5 — Serge Prokofieff - CONCERTO NO. 3, p. 35 l. 1 m. 4, l. 2 m. 1
Used by permission of Leeds Music Corporation, New York, Copyright Owners

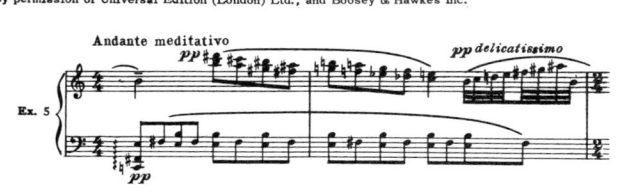

Copyright 1923 Breitkopf and Härtel (A. Gutheil)
Copyright assigned 1947 Boosey & Hawkes Ltd.

FOR REFERENCE:

Debussy - JARDINS SOUS LA PLUIE, Dd, p. 18 l. 4 & 5
Scott - LOTUSLAND, Elk, p. 6 l. 1 & 3
Debussy - FANTASY (Piano and Orchestra), Fr, p. 42 l. 2
Bloch - CONCERTO SYMPHONIQUE, B & H, p. 43 m. 4-5
Turel - TWELVE SKETCHES, Leeds, p. 11
Shostakovitch - CONCERTO op. 35, Leeds, p. 59 l. 1 m. 2-3

II
The Modes Applied in Modern Music

All these Modes could be transposed by starting them on any degree of the chromatic scale.

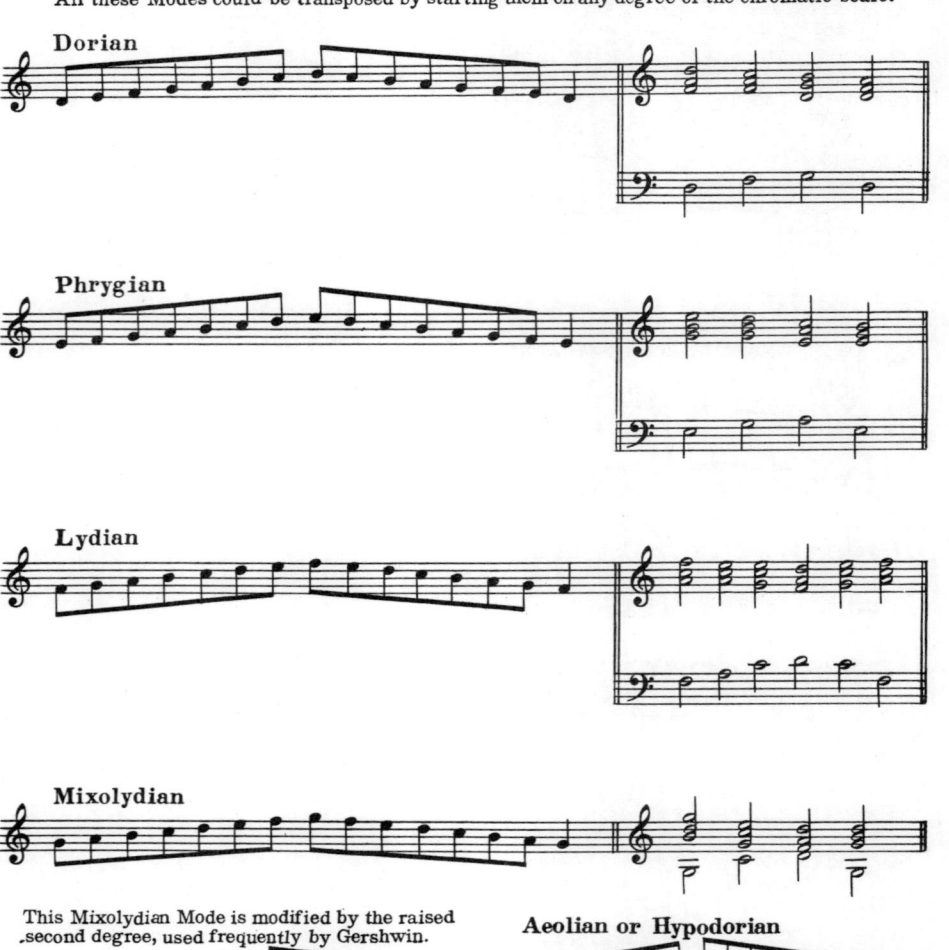

Dorian

Phrygian

Lydian

Mixolydian

This Mixolydian Mode is modified by the raised second degree, used frequently by Gershwin.

Aeolian or Hypodorian

© Copyright 1960 by SOUTHERN MUSIC PUBLISHING COMPANY, INC.
International Copyright Secured   Printed in U. S. A.
All Rights Reserved Including the Right of Public Performance for Profit

Ex. 1

Paul Hindemith - LUDUS TONALIS, p. 1 l. 2 m. 1 (Phrygian)
Copyright 1943 by Schott & Co., Ltd.
Used by permission of Associated Music Publishers, Inc., New York

Ex. 2

Luis Gianneo - SONATINA, p. 4 l. 4 m. 4, l. 5, l. 6 m. 1-3
Used by permission of Editorial Argentina de Musica, Buenos Aires
Sole Representatives: Southern Music Publishing Company, Inc., New York

Ex. 3

Ned Rorem - CONCERTO NO. 2, p. 1 m. 1-8
Used by permission of Southern Music Publishing Company, Inc., New York

Ex. 4 Allegro
p dolce

Anis Fuleihan - SONATA NO. 2, p. 3 l. 3 m. 1-5 (Hypodorian)
Used by permission of Southern Music Publishing Company, Inc., New York, Copyright Owners

Ex. 5 *con molta forza*
poco ped.

poco allarg.   *con tutta forza*

Peter Mennin - TOCCATA (from Five Piano Pieces), p. 31 l. 2 m. 3-4, l. 3-5
Copyright © 1951 by Carl Fischer, Inc., New York
International Copyright Secured
Used by permission of Carl Fischer, Inc.

FOR REFERENCE:

Debussy - LA CATHEDRALE ENGLOUTIE, Dd
     CANOPE, Dd
Casella - ELEVEN PIECES FOR CHILDREN, U.E., p. 12
Respighi - THREE PRELUDES ON GREGORIAN CHANTS, U.E.
Gershwin - RHAPSODY IN BLUE, Harms, p. 4 (Aeolian & Mixolydian)
     PRELUDE NO. 2, Harms
Bloch - CHANTY (from Poems of the Sea), Schr., l. 1-2
Chavez - TEN PRELUDES, Schr. (album), p. 252, l. 1-3
Read - PETITE PASTORALE op. 40, Summy
Green - PASTORALE (No. 5 from Festival Fugues), Arrow
Hanson - CONCERTO op. 36, C.F., first movement in full
Prokofieff - CONCERTO NO. 5, Leeds, p. 14 (Aeolian)
     SONATA NO. 3, Leeds, p. 5 l. 4&5 (Dorian)
Shostakovitch - TWENTY FOUR PRELUDES, Leeds, No. 1 p. 8 (Aeolian)
     CONCERTO op. 35, Leeds, p. 29 l. 2 m. 1-4 (Phrygian)

IIIA
The Pentatonic Scales

  To be started on any of its five tones and extended over several octaves.
 The first models show an all-black-key row. You may transpose these tones on any of the 12 tones within the octave.

A   B   C   D

1

2

3

© Copyright 1960 by SOUTHERN MUSIC PUBLISHING COMPANY, INC.
International Copyright Secured   Printed in U. S. A.
All Rights Reserved Including the Right of Public Performance for Profit

Poco meno mosso

Ex. 1

Serge Prokofieff - CONCERTO NO. 3, p. 20 l. 3 m. 1-2
Used by permission of Leeds Music Corporation, New York, Copyright Owners

Copyright 1923 Breitkopf and Härtel (A. Gutheil)
Copyright assigned 1947 Boosey & Hawkes Ltd.

Andante cantabile piu lento ♩ = 72

Ex. 2

Ray Green - TWELVE INVENTIONS, p. 25 l. 1 & 2, l. 3 m. 1-2
Copyright 1956 by American Music Edition, New York
Used by permission of American Music Edition

FOR REFERENCE:

Debussy - CHILDREN'S CORNER, II. "Jumbo's Lullaby", Dd
PAGODES, Dd, p. 1
Scott - LOTUSLAND, Elk, p. 5 in full
Tcherepnine - THREE CONCERT ETUDES op. 52, Schott
Read - AMERICAN CIRCLE, Summy

III.B
Black and White Keys in Contrast

The whole-tone scales and triads in contrasting combinations

1.

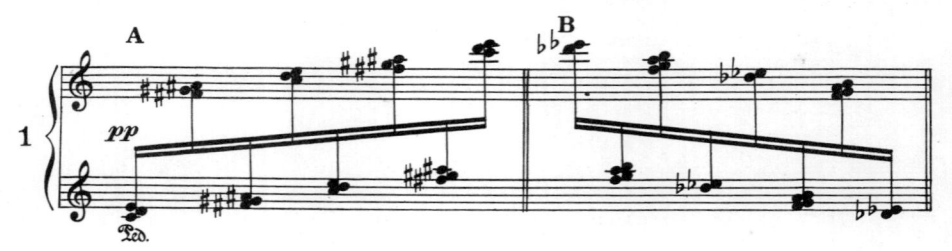

Cluster- technique.   See C VIII.

This combination of triads on black and white keys is used by the French School, Impressionists, and in particular by M. Ravel.   See example "Jeux d'eau."

2. A To be played over several octaves

B   C

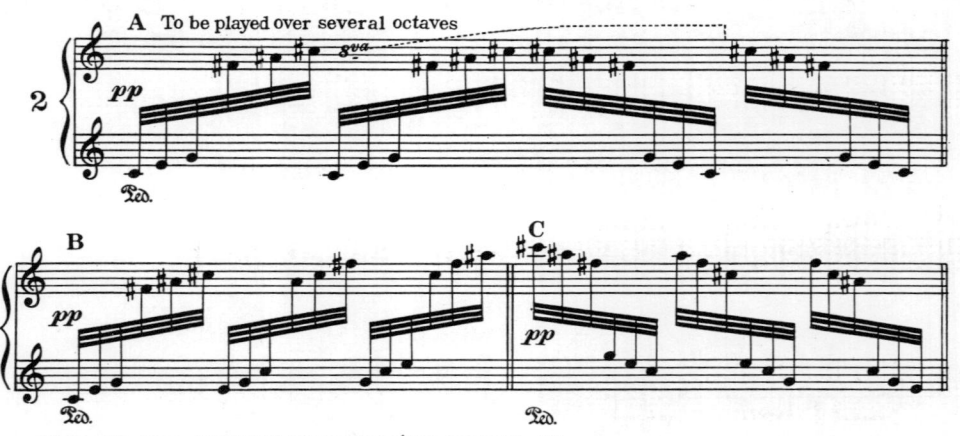

© Copyright 1960 by SOUTHERN MUSIC PUBLISHING COMPANY, INC.
International Copyright Secured   Printed in U. S. A.
All Rights Reserved Including the Right of Public Performance for Profit

Italian School (Casella, Malipiero, etc.)
Diatonic white-key progressions trimmed with black keys.

© Copyright 1960 by SOUTHERN MUSIC PUBLISHING COMPANY, INC.
International Copyright Secured Printed in U.S.A.
All Rights Reserved Including the Right of Public Performance for Profit

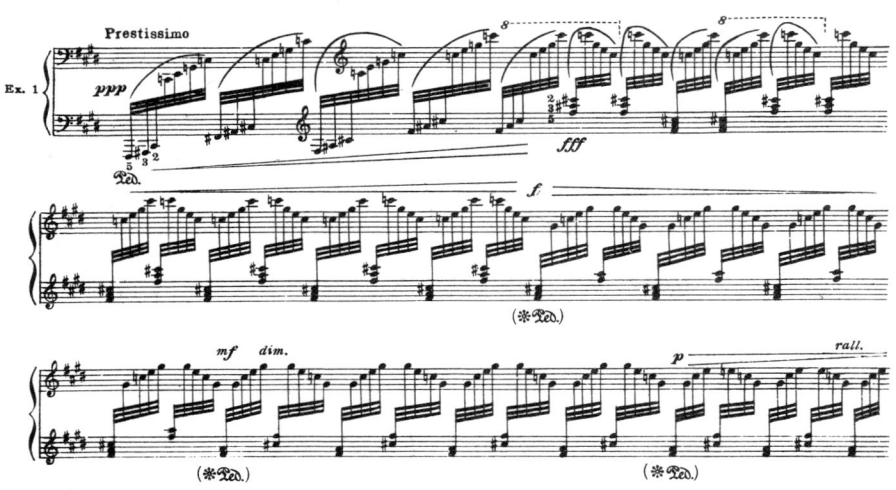

Maurice Ravel - JEUX D'EAU, p. 13 l. 2-4
Used by permission of B. F. Wood Music Company

Paul Hindemith - LUDUS TONALIS, p. 38 l. 3 m. 1-3, l. 4 m. 2-3
Copyright 1943 by Schott & Co., Ltd.
Used by permission of Associated Music Publishers, Inc., New York

Molto allegro

Ex. 3

Robert Starer - FIVE CAPRICES, No. 5, p. 10 l. 2 m. 2-4, l. 3 m. 1-3
Used by permission of Peer International Corporation, New York, Copyright Owners

Ex. 4

Samuel Barber - SONATA op. 26, p. 10 l. 3 m. 2
Copyright 1950 by G. Schirmer, Inc., International Copyright Secured
Used by permission of G. Schirmer, Inc.

Ex. 5 Serge Prokofieff - CONCERTO NO. 3, p. 20 l. 3 m. 1-2 (see IIIA, Ex. 1)

FOR REFERENCE:

Debussy - BROUILLARDS, Dd
          FEUX D'ARTIFICE, Dd, first 3 pages
Casella - ELEVEN PIECES FOR CHILDREN, U.E., No. 1, No. 9
Gershwin - CONCERTO IN F, Harms, 3rd mvt., last 4 m.
Villa-Lobos - RUDEPOEMA, Esch., p. 15
Slonimsky - STUDIES IN BLACK AND WHITE, NM
Honegger - CONCERTINO, Senart, p. 4 l. 1
Bartók - OUT DOORS, U.E., "Barcarolla"
       MIKROKOSMOS, B & H, Vol. 6, "Diary of the Fly", p. 9
Milhaud - TOUCHES BLANCHES ET TOUCHES NOIRES, C.F.
Bowles - FOLK PRELUDES, Mercury, p. 5, l. 5 & 6
Chaim - SONATA, Leeds, p. 3 l. 4 & 5, p. 7 l. 3 & 4
Prokofieff - SONATA NO. 7, Leeds, p. 12 l. 1-3, p. 26 l. 3 m. 3-4
Khachaturian - CONCERTO, Leeds, p. 35 l. 1 m. 1-3, p. 72 l. 1, l. 2 m. 1-2

IIIc

The Sixte ajoutée

Cadence with applied "Sixte ajoutée." Transpose this cadence into various keys, in different positions and also in broken chords with variations. See: Ray Green, Sonata Brevis; Gershwin, Preludes, where the modal key with its shifting major and minor thirds is distinctly shown.

© Copyright 1960 by SOUTHERN MUSIC PUBLISHING COMPANY, INC.
International Copyright Secured   Printed in U.S.A.
All Rights Reserved Including the Right of Public Performance for Profit

Heitor Villa-Lobos - GUIA PRATICO, p. 2 l. 4 m. 3, l. 5 m. 1-3
Used by permission of Southern Music Publishing Company, Inc., New York, Copyright Owners

Ray Green - TWELVE INVENTIONS, p. 31, l. 4-6
Copyright 1956 by American Music Edition, New York
Used by permission of American Music Edition

FOR REFERENCE:

Debussy - FEUX D'ARTIFICE, Dd, p. 4&5
FANTASY (Piano and Orchestra), Fr, 1st mvt.
Gershwin - RHAPSODY IN BLUE, Harms, p. 6 l. 3
PRELUDE NO. 1, Harms
CONCERTO IN F, Harms, p. 19 l. 4, p. 20 l. 1-4

IVA

Bi-tonal Combinations of Major and Minor Scales

To be played in four octaves, both directions.
Use conventional fingering of the scales.
This pattern is a combination of C major, admitting 8 combinations.
It should be combined with any of the twelve major keys.
If wanted, likewise in the twelve minor scales (harmonic.)

Bi-tonal passages in Chromatic Order

As preparatory exercise play first the right hand in unison with the left hand.

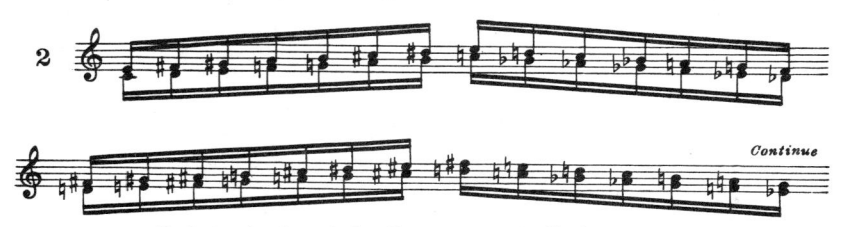

Exchange hands and play these passages in Sixths.

© Copyright 1960 by SOUTHERN MUSIC PUBLISHING COMPANY, INC.
International Copyright Secured   Printed in U. S. A.
All Rights Reserved Including the Right of Public Performance for Profit

Ex. 1

Francis Poulenc - FIVE IMPROMPTUS, p. 2 l. 1 m. 2, p. 9 l. 2 m. 3&4
Used by permission of J. & W. Chester, Ltd., London

Ex. 2

Paul Hindemith - SECOND SONATA, p. 14 l. 1 m. 4-6
Copyright 1936 by B. Schott's Soehne, Mainz
Used by permission of Associated Music Publishers, Inc., New York

Ex. 3 Prestissimo ♩ = 184

Alexandre Tcherepnine - BAGATELLES op. 5, p. 17 l. 4 m. 1-8
Used by permission of the International Music Company, New York, Copyright

Ex. 4 Allegro marcato

Serge Prokofieff - TOCCATA op. 11, p. 7 l. 2-3
Used by permission of Leeds Music Corporation, New York, Copyright Owners

FOR REFERENCE:

Piston - CONCERTINO, p. 7 m. 9-10, p. 8 m. 8-14
Prokofieff - SARCASMES, No. 3 op. 17
Ives - SONATA NO. 2 (Concord), Arrow, p. 7 l. 1
Gianneo - SONATINA, EAM, p. 8 l. 4
Thomson - NINE ETUDES, C.F., No. 3
Shostakovitch - CONCERTO op. 35, Leeds, p. 38 l. 3 m. 2-5, p. 39 l. 1 m. 1-2

IV B

Bi tonal and Polytonal Combinations of Triads and other Chords

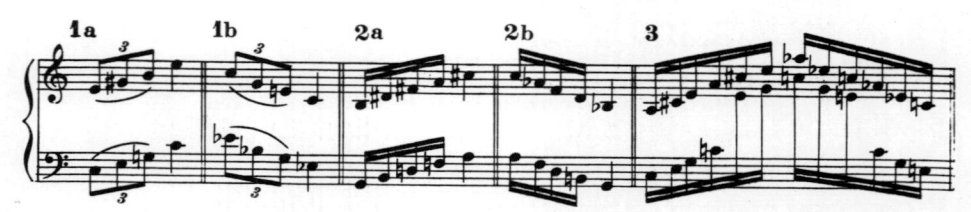

1a   1b   2a   2b   3

Each of these patterns should be played through several octaves and can be started on any pair of keys.

Major and Minor Triads in progression of the Diminished Seventh-Chord. Left hand one Octave lower. To be started at any tone of the Chromatic Scale. Play also in broken progression; Three- or Four-parted Triads could be used.

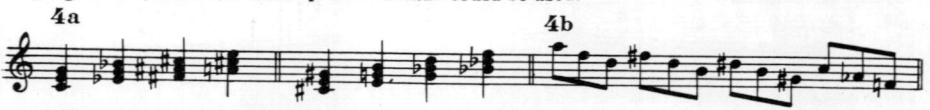

4a   4b

© Copyright 1960 by SOUTHERN MUSIC PUBLISHING COMPANY, INC.
International Copyright Secured   Printed in U.S.A.
All Rights Reserved Including the Right of Public Performance for Profit

Bi tonal Combinations of two Diminished Seventh Chords

5a **5b**

To be played through several octaves in both directions.

The simultaneous use of the 3 Diminished Seventh-Chords in Major Thirds-spacing, resulting in Augmented Triads. Play first two parts, lower or upper parts; then all three, resulting in Augmented Triads. Start also one half tone higher, then another half tone higher.

6

continue

Folktune harmonized with Augmented Triads. This rigid usage of the identical Harmonies could be applied on any other tune and should serve for practicing the habit.

7

continue

Both Whole-tone Scales in Bi tonal progression

8a **8b** **8c** **8d**

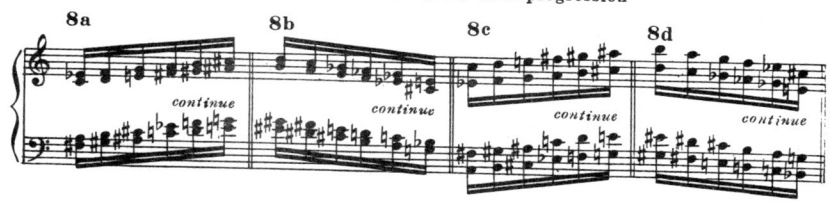

continue *continue* *continue* *continue*

Polytonal model. Observe the Four Major Scales:
C, A flat, D and B flat, as they procede.

9a **9b** **9c** **9d**

continue *continue*

Use this, or any other simple melody as Exercise for Polytonality. Start at any tone and make the combination within the Diminished Seventh-chord.

10

continue

© Copyright 1960 by SOUTHERN MUSIC PUBLISHING COMPANY, INC.
International Copyright Secured   Printed in U.S.A.
All Rights Reserved Including the Right of Public Performance for Profit

Ex. 1

sost. Ped.

f suddenly   *ff*

sost. Ped. off

Gail Kubik - SONATA, p. 19 l. 3 m. 3, l. 4 m. 1-4
Used by permission of Southern Music Publishing Company, Inc., New York, Copyright Owners

Ex. 2

Gottfried von Einem - TWO SONATINAS, p. 10 l. 1 m. 3-4, l. 2, l. 3 m. 1-3
Copyright 1950 by Universal Edition, Vienna
Used by permission of Associated Music Publishers, Inc., New York

Ex. 3

Rodolfo Halffter - SECOND SONATA, p. 5 l. 1-3, l. 4 m. 1-4
Used by permission of Pan American Union, Washington, D.C.
Sole Representatives: Peer International Corporation, New York

Ex. 4

Dmitri Kabalevsky - SONATA NO. 3, p. 3 l. 1-3
Used by permission of Leeds Music Corporation, New York, Copyright Owners

FOR REFERENCE:

Debussy - FEUILLES MORTS, Dd
Satie - DESCRIPTIONS AUTOMATIQUES, Esch., No. 3, p. 7&8
Gershwin - CONCERTO IN F, Harms, p. 8 l. 1-2
Kodaly - DANCES OF MAROSZEK, U.E.
Tcherepnine - BAGATELLES op. 5, IMC, p. 16 l. 4 m. 9-11
Thomson - PORTRAITS, Mercury, "Bugles and Birds", "Tango Lullaby"
Milhaud - CONCERTO NO. 3, AMP, p. 8, p. 14, p. 28
Martinu - CONCERTO FOR TWO PIANOS (with orchestra), AMP

Vₐ
Bi tonal Combinations of the Two Whole-tone Scales

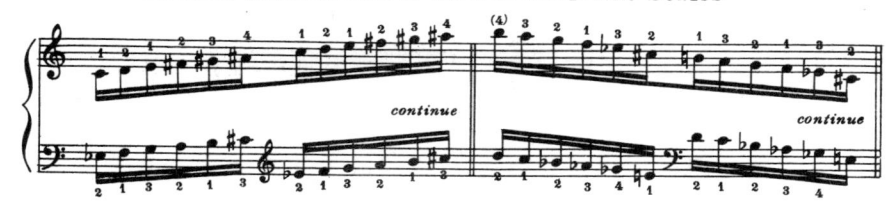

© Copyright 1960 by SOUTHERN MUSIC PUBLISHING COMPANY, INC.
International Copyright Secured   Printed in U. S. A.
All Rights Reserved Including the Right of Public Performance for Profit

Ex. 1

Paul Hindemith - FIRST SONATA, p. 5 m. 9-12
Copyright 1936 by B. Schott's Soehne, Mainz
Used by permission of Associated Music Publishers, Inc., New York

Ex. 2

Béla Bartók - THIRD CONCERTO, p. 23 l. 2&3, p. 36 l. 3, p. 41 l. 2 m. 2
Copyright 1947 by Hawkes & Son (London) Ltd.
Used by permission of Boosey & Hawkes Inc.

V_B
Bi tonal Combinations of Major, Minor, and Augmented Triads, as well as other Chords, within the Whole-tone Scales

Major and Minor Triads in Whole-tone progression. Play in both directions, up and down, also broken and with both hands. The Melody below is harmonized with all Major Triads. It can be harmonized with all Minor or all Augmented Triads.

Use any other simple tune for such experiments

1a   1b   1c

1d   2

continue

© Copyright 1960 by SOUTHERN MUSIC PUBLISHING COMPANY, INC.
International Copyright Secured   Printed in U. S. A.
All Rights Reserved Including the Right of Public Performance for Profit

Augmented Triads in Bitonal Combinations

3a

3b

© Copyright 1960 by SOUTHERN MUSIC PUBLISHING COMPANY, INC.
International Copyright Secured   Printed in U.S.A.
All Rights Reserved Including the Right of Public Performance for Profit

Ex. 1

Jose Ardévol - SONATA NO. 3, p. 2 l. 5 m. 3-5, p. 3 l. 1 m. 1-5, l. 2 m. 1-2
Used by permission of Editorial Cooperativa Interamericana de Compositores, Montevideo
Sole Representatives: Southern Music Publishing Company, Inc., New York

Ex. 2

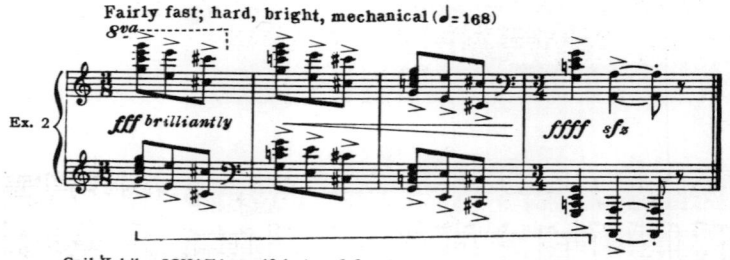

Gail Kubik - SONATA, p. 40 l. 4 m. 3-6
Used by permission of Southern Music Publishing Company, Inc., New York, Copyright Owners

Ex. 3

Serge Prokofieff - CONCERTO NO. 3, p. 32 l. 1 m. 1-3
Used by permission of Leeds Music Corporation, New York, Copyright Owners

Copyright 1923 Breitkopf and Härtel (A. Gutheil)
Copyright assigned 1947 Boosey & Hawkes Ltd.

FOR REFERENCE:

Ravel - JEUX D'EAU, Wood, p. 6 l. 3-4
Debussy - REFLETS DANS L'EAU, Dd, p. 2 l. 2
         GENERAL LAVINE ECCENTRIC, Dd
Pisk - FIVE SKETCHES, N.M., No. 3, p. 14 l. 1-2
Hindemith - LUDUS TONALIS, AMP, p. 7 l. 2 m. 3, l. 3 m. 1
Bloch - SONATA, Carisch, p. 17 l. 1-3
Leighton - SECOND SONATA, Mills

VI A
Dislocations of Traditional Harmonic Relations, "Twisted Cadences" and other Alterations

The Cadence with lowered or raised Dominants. Such Alterations of the Principal Harmonies should serve as Exercise for Compositions with similar deviations within the Cadence.

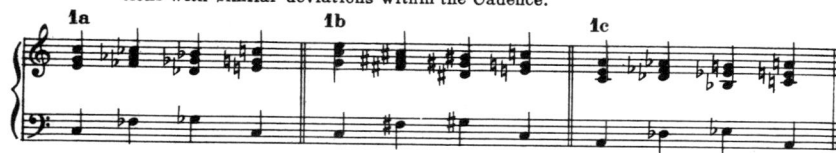

1a **1b** **1c**

Observe the Cadence-Harmonies in this simple tune, and experiment with other melodies, likewise applying Altered Dominants.

2

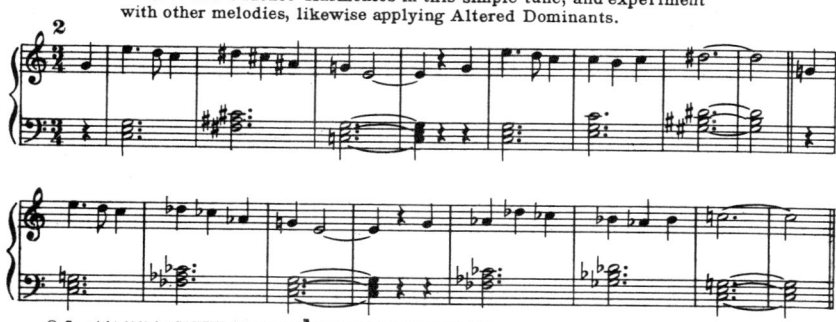

© Copyright 1960 by SOUTHERN MUSIC PUBLISHING COMPANY, INC.
International Copyright Secured   Printed in U. S. A.
All Rights Reserved Including the Right of Public Performance for Profit

Ex. 1 ♩=66
una corda
Roy Harris - LITTLE SUITE, p. 5 "Slumber", l. 1
Copyright 1939 by G. Schirmer, Inc., International Copyright Secured
Used by permission of G. Schirmer, Inc.

Ex. 2 Rondo ♩=120

Rondó ♩=120
Rodolfo Halffter - SECOND SONATA, p. 32 l. 1 m. 1-3, l. 5 m. 2-4
Used by permission of Pan American Union, Washington, D.C.
Sole Representatives: Peer International Corporation, New York

Ex. 3 Allegro

Serge Prokofieff - CONCERTO NO. 3, p. 5 l. 2 m. 3, l. 3 m. 1-3
Used by permission of Leeds Music Corporation, New York, Copyright Owners

Copyright 1923 Breitkopf and Härtel (A. Gutheil)
Copyright assigned 1947 Boosey & Hawkes Ltd.

FOR REFERENCE:

Debussy - LES FÉES SONT D'EXQUISES DANSEUSES, Dd
          LA TERRASSA DES AUDIENCES DU CLAIR DE LUNE, Dd
Bartók - TEN EASY PIECES, "Bear Dance"
Feinberg - SONATA NO. 6 op. 13, U.E.
Gershwin - CONCERTO IN F, Harms, p. 6
Auric - SONATA IN F, Lerolle, 1st mvt & p. 10 l. 3 & 4, 4th mvt
Harris - LITTLE SUITE, Schr., p. 4 "Sad News"
Bloch - VISIONS AND PROPHECIES, Schr., p. 6 l. 3-4, p. 7 l. 1-2, p. 12, l. 3-5
Mompou - DANZA NO. 2, Espanola
Creston - PRELUDE AND DANCE op. 29/1, Mercury, p. 5
J.M. Castro - SONATA DE PRIMAVERA, EAM, p. 14
Stravinsky - TANGO, Mercury
Hindemith - LUDUS TONALIS, AMP, p. 12 l. 6 m. 4-5
Wash. Castro - INTERMEZZO NO. 1, EAM, p. 2-4
Bacon - TEN PIECES, Schr., "Maple Sugaring"
Khachaturian - CONCERTO, Leeds, p. 29 l. 2 m. 3, l. 3, p. 46 l. 3 m. 2-3, p. 47 l. 1, l. 2 m. 1
Wordworth - CONCERTO, A. Lengnick
Chagrin - CONCERTO, A. Lengnick
Egk - SONATA, Schott, p. 4, p. 7 l. 4-5, p. 9, p. 12
Shostakovitch - TWENTY FOUR PRELUDES, Leeds, No.'s 6, 7, 9, 10, 12, 24
Harris - AMERICAN BALLADES, C.F.
Kabalevsky - SONATA NO. 3, Leeds, p. 3 l. 1-3
             CONCERTO NO. 3, Leeds, p. 29 l. 1 m. 1-4
Prokofieff - SONATA NO. 3, Leeds, p. 3, p. 10 l. 3 m. 1-2, l. 4 m. 1-2, p. 16 l. 4-5
             SONATA NO. 7, Leeds, p. 22 l. 3

VI_B
Polytonality through passages and through "Telescoping" Harmonies. (*zusammengeschoben*)

Ex. 1 — **Im Zeitmass**

Paul Hindemith - SECOND SONATA, p. 4 l. 1 m. 1-4
Copyright 1936 by B. Schott's Soehne, Mainz
Used by permission of the Associated Music Publishers, Inc., New York

Ex. 2

William Schuman - CONCERTO, p. 22 l. 2
Copyright 1943 by G. Schirmer, Inc., International Copyright Secured
Used by permission of G. Schirmer, Inc.

Ex. 3 — **Tempo di Minuetto un poco mosso**

Luis Gianneo - SONATINA, p. 10 l. 1 m. 2-5, l. 2 m. 1
Used by permission of Editorial Argentina de Musica, Buenos Aires
Sole Representatives: Southern Music Publishing Company, Inc., New York

Ex. 4 — **Moderately fast, gracefully** ($\quarter = 84$)

Gaily (in 2 - $\half = 92$)
p smoothly, but with sharp rhythm throughout

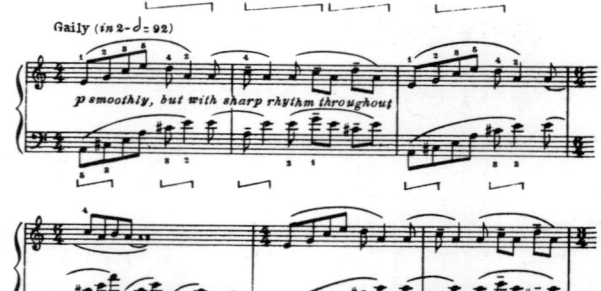

Gail Kubik - SONATA, p. 6 l. 1 m. 1-4, l. 3 m. 1-3, p. 14 l. 1 m. 1-3, l. 2
Used by permission of Southern Music Publishing Company, Inc., New York, Copyright Owners

FOR REFERENCE:

Bartók - SUITE op. 14, U.E., p. 18
Szymanowski - MAZURKAS op. 50, U.E., No. 2
               MASQUES op. 34, U.E., No. 1
Bartók - ALLEGRO BARBARO, U.E.
Wellesz - FÜNF TANZSTÜCKE, U.E., No. 4
Toch - TEN CONCERT STUDIES, Schott, No.'s 1 & 6
       PROFILES op. 68, AMP
Luening - EIGHT PRELUDES, N.M., No.'s 1 & 6
Bloch - SONATA, Carisch, p. 3 l. 1-3, p. 11 l. 2-3
Bowles - SIX PRELUDES, Mercury
Tansman - INTERMEZZI, Esch., No. 3 & 5
Darnton - CONCERTINO, Mills
Harris - TOCCATA, C.F.
v. Einem - TWO SONATINAS, U.E., p. 17 l. 1-3
Reizenstein - TWELVE PRELUDES AND FUGUES, Mills
Dello Joio - THIRD SONATA, C.F., p. 8-9
Helm - TOCCATA BRASILEIRA, C.F.
Shostakovitch - CONCERTO op. 35, Leeds, p. 8 l. 2 m. 3, l. 3 m. 1-2, p. 15 l. 2 m. 2,
       l. 3 m. 1-2, p. 34 l. 3 m. 2, l. 4 m. 1-2, l. 5 m. 1, p. 60 l. 4 m. 3-6
      POLKA op. 22
      SONATA NO. 2, Leeds, 1st mvt (Telescoping)
Prokofieff - SONATA NO. 9, Leeds, p. 10 l. 5 m. 1-2, p. 19 l. 2 m. 2
      TOCCATA, Leeds, p. 4 l. 2-3, p. 6 l. 1-3

VII A
Expansions and Contractions of the Traditional Scales

Diatonic Scales, Expanded over Two Octaves, progressing in Thirds.
1) Major Scales in Chromatic progression, Zig-zag motion.

Play also in Diatonic progression in one direction; Transpose into different Keys
2) Minor Scales in Diatonic progression, Zig-zag motion

Transpose into other Minor Scales

Chromatic, perfect fourths in straight progression. The other hand, "Covering" the fourths, plays the Chromatic Scale divided into two octaves, alternatingly, whereby the fifth finger is playing one Whole-tone scale, while the first finger is playing the other Whole-tone scale. It should be played in several octaves in both directions. Such a division of the Chromatic Scale is the first step to the trend of expansion of intervals in new music.

3a   3b   3c   3d   3e

Expansion of the Chromatic Scale with Contraction of Triads.

4a

4b

© Copyright 1960 by SOUTHERN MUSIC PUBLISHING COMPANY, INC.
International Copyright Secured   Printed in U.S.A.
All Rights Reserved Including the Right of Public Performance for Profit

Arnold Schoenberg - FIVE PIANO PIECES op. 23, p. 15 l. 3 m. 3, l. 4 m. 1-2
Copyright 1923 - 1951 by Wilhelm Hansen, Copenhagen
Used by permission of the Publishers

Ex. 2

Serge Prokofieff - SONATA NO. 7, p. 9 l. 2 m. 2-3, l. 3 m. 1-2
Used by permission of Leeds Music Corporation, New York, Copyright Owners

Ex. 3

Juan Carlos Paz - THIRD SONATINA, p. 5 l. 3-4
Used by permission of Editorial Cooperativa Interamericana de Compositores, Montevideo
Sole Representatives: Southern Music Publishing Company, Inc., New York

FOR REFERENCE:

    Feinberg - SONATA NO. 6, U.E.
    Hindemith - LUDUS TONALIS, AMP, p. 18 l. 3 m. 2-3, l. 4 m. 1-2 (left hand only),
        p. 30 l. 2 m. 2-3, l. 3 m. 1
    Shostakovitch - TWENTY FOUR PRELUDES, Leeds, No. 5
    Slonimsky - THESAURUS OF SCALES AND MELODIC PATTERNS, Coleman-Ross
    Kubik - SONATA, SMPC, p. 14 m. 1-3
    Tcherepnine - EXPRESSIONS, Leeds, p. 5 l. 1-2, p. 17
    Scriabin - SONATA NO. 5, Leeds, m. 1-11
        SONATA NO. 7, Leeds
    Khachaturian - CONCERTO, Leeds, p. 7 l. 2 m. 3-4, l. 3 m. 1-2

VII B
Expansions and Contractions of Intervals:
Thirds, Sixths and as Diminished Octaves, the Sevenths

Start on any tone of the Chromatic Scale, each hand alone, also both hands together, the left hand one or two Octaves lower. Also play with both hands, the left hand a Minor Sixth, a Major sixth, a Minor Third, or a Major Third lower, in positions as shown in Sketches **1b**, **1c**, **1d**, **1e**. The Thirds are played one Octave lower (in Tenths) in order to avoid crowding of hands.

Sketches for l.h. in combination with r.h.

© Copyright 1960 by SOUTHERN MUSIC PUBLISHING COMPANY, INC.
International Copyright Secured   Printed in U.S.A.
All Rights Reserved Including the Right of Public Performance for Profit

Chromatic progression distributed in Major Sevenths. Construct the same pattern in Minor Sevenths within the Whole-tone Scales.

© Copyright 1960 by SOUTHERN MUSIC PUBLISHING COMPANY, INC.
International Copyright Secured   Printed in U.S.A.
All Rights Reserved Including the Right of Public Performance for Profit

Ex. 1

Charles E. Ives - FIRST SONATA, p. 29 l. 1, l. 2 m. 1-2
Used by permission of Peer International Corporation, New York, Copyright Owners

Ex. 2 Acalanto ($\quarternote = 54-58$)

Heitor Villa-Lobos - GUIA PRATICO, p. 6 m. 1-4
Used by permission of Southern Music Publishing Company, Inc., New York, Copyright Owners

Rodolfo Halffter - SECOND SONATA, p. 5 l. 4 m. 5-6, l. 5
Used by permission of Pan American Union, Washington, D.C.
Sole Representatives: Peer International Corporation, New York

FOR REFERENCE:

Schoenberg - DREI KLAVIERSTÜCKE op. 11, U.E.
Debussy - LES TIERCES ALTERNEES, Dd
Toch - TEN RECITAL STUDIES, Schott, No.'s 2, 7, 8
Tansman - INTERMEZZI, AMP, No.'s 1 & 6
    SONATA NO. 4, AMP
    INTERMEZZI, Esch., No.'s 1 & 2
Copland - VARIATIONS, Cos. Cob Press, p. 5 m. 9, p. 6 up to rehearsal 8
Bartók - MIKROKOSMOS, B&H, Vol. 6, p. 13, p. 14, p. 15
   CONCERTO NO. 3, B&H, p. 69 l. 2 m. 3-6, l. 3 m. 1-4
Jolivet - FIVE RITUAL DANCES, Dd
Shostakovitch - TWENTY FOUR PRELUDES, Leeds, No.'s 17 & 19
     SONATA NO. 2, Leeds, p. 18, p. 23
Ives - SONATA NO. 2 (Concord), Arrow, p. 3 l. 4
Scriabin - SONATA NO. 5, Leeds
   SONATA NO. 6, Leeds m. 1-16
   SONATA NO. 7, Leeds
Prokofieff - SONATA NO. 7, Leeds, p. 9 l. 3-4
Khachaturian - CONCERTO, Leeds, p. 55 l. 2 m. 1-2
Krenek - GEORGE WASHINGTON VARIATIONS, SMPC, p. 13 l. 2 m. 2-3, l. 3 m. 1-2
Green - TWELVE INVENTIONS, AME, p. 17 l. 1-2

VII c

Expansions and Contractions of Harmonic Structures

© Copyright 1960 by SOUTHERN MUSIC PUBLISHING COMPANY, INC.
International Copyright Secured   Printed in U.S.A.
All Rights Reserved Including the Right of Public Performance for Profit

Lower whole-tone expansion

Lower whole-tone contraction

Left hand Two Octaves lower, either alone or in unison with r.h.
to be transposed into all Major and Minor Keys.

© Copyright 1960 by SOUTHERN MUSIC PUBLISHING COMPANY, INC.
International Copyright Secured   Printed in U.S.A.
All Rights Reserved Including the Right of Public Performance for Profit

Ex. 1

Arnold Schoenberg - FIVE PIANO PIECES op. 23, p. 4 l. 1-2
Copyright 1923 - 1951 by Wilhelm Hansen, Copenhagen
Used by permission of the Publishers

Ex. 2

Aaron Copland - SONATA, p. 4 l. 5 m. 1-3
Copyright 1942 by Boosey & Hawkes Inc.
Used by permission of Boosey & Hawkes Inc.

Ex. 3

Aram Khachaturian - CONCERTO, p. 27 l. m. 3, l. 2
Used by permission of Leeds Music Corporation, New York, Copyright Owners

FOR REFERENCE:

Schoenberg - DREI KLAVIERSTÜCKE op. 11, U.E.
Jolivet - FIVE RITUAL DANCES, Dd
Toch - IDEAS, Delkas, p. 8, p. 12
Hanson - ENCHANTMENT, C.F.
Tcherepnine - EXPRESSIONS, Leeds, p. 9
Krenek - SONATA NO. 2, U.E., 3rd mvt
Shostakovitch - SONATA NO. 2, Leeds

VII D
Expansions and Contractions
Melody Deviations (*Irregular Progressions*)

Chromatic chain of the diatonic scales with seven steps only.
To be played in Minor Scales too. Left hand either alternating with
right hand or one octave lower. Play also downwards.

Expansions and Contractions of Harmonic Structures as Reflected in Melody Deviation.

These samples could be played in several octaves.
The short patterns could also be used as sequences and played in
several octaves. The player should try to add variety by inversion and change of direction of the given patterns.
The models could be played unison with both hands, one or two
octaves apart.

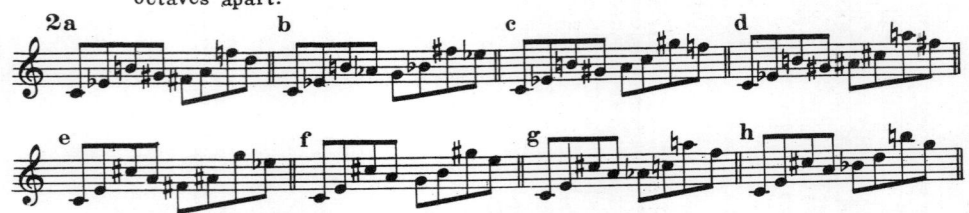

Igor Strawinsky - CONCERTO FOR PIANO AND WIND INSTRUMENTS, p. 11 m. 4-7
Copyright 1924 by Edition Russe de Musique; Renewed 1952
Copyright and Renewal assigned to Boosey & Hawkes Ltd.
Used by permission of Boosey & Hawkes Inc.

Paul Hindemith - SECOND SONATA, p. 10 l. 1 m. 6, l. 2 m. 1-5
Copyright 1936 by B. Schott's Soehne, Mainz
Used by permission of Associated Music Publishers, Inc., New York

Ray Green - FESTIVAL FUGUES, "An American Toccata", p. 11 l. 4, p. 12 l. 1
Copyright 1949 by Arrow Music Press, Inc.
Copyright assigned to American Music Edition, New York, N.Y.
Used by permission of American Music Edition

FOR REFERENCE:

Schoenberg - DREI KLAVIERSTÜCKE op. 11, U.E.
Bartók - OUT DOORS, U.E., "Barcarolla", p. 8
Toch - TEN CONCERT STUDIES, Schott, No. 5
Slonimsky - THESAURUS OF SCALES AND MELODIC PATTERNS, Coleman-Ross
Schoenberg - KLAVIERSTÜCK op. 33 A, U.E., p. 6
Ives - SONATA NO. 2 (Concord), Arrow, p. 32
Prokofieff - SONATA NO. 3, Leeds, p. 7 l. 3 m. 3-4
Shostakovitch - CONCERTO op. 35, Leeds, p. 34 l. 1 m. 1-2, l. 2 m. 1

VIII A
Chords and Progressions of Fourths and Fifths

Chords in perfect Fourths in Chromatic Progression. These chords could be expanded from 6-parted to 8 or 10-parted chords by adding a lower and an upper fourth to each chord. These chords could be played as chords or arpeggios. To be constructed with augmented fourths in some of the parts, at your will. Play also downward.

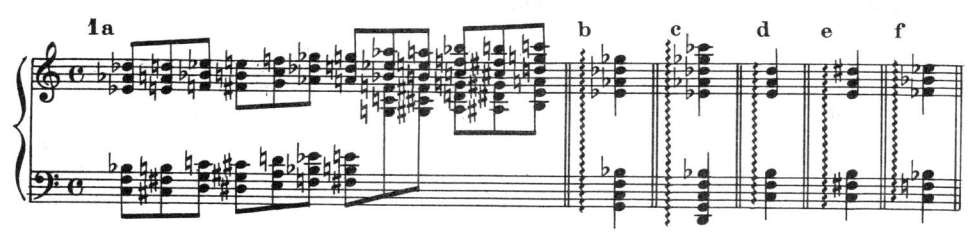

If these chords are played broken, the directions of the arpeggios could alternate: first upward, the next chord downward, a.s.o.

Chords in Fourths within a Diatonic Progression

The Major and Minor Key of the two examples above have been chosen at random. Transpose the models into other Major and Minor Keys.

Symmetrical exchange of Fourths and Fifths

non legato

transpose chromatically

transpose chromatically

© Copyright 1960 by SOUTHERN MUSIC PUBLISHING COMPANY, INC.
International Copyright Secured Printed in U.S.A.
All Rights Reserved Including the Right of Public Performance for Profit

26

© Copyright 1960 by SOUTHERN MUSIC PUBLISHING COMPANY, INC.
International Copyright Secured   Printed in U. S. A.
All Rights Reserved Including the Right of Public Performance for Profit

Ex. 1

Ernst Krenek - SECOND PIANO SONATA, p. 3 l. 3
Copyright 1928 by Associated Music Publishers, Inc., New York; Renewed 1956
Used by permission of Associated Music Publishers, Inc.

Ex. 2

* S.P. = Sustaining Pedal
Roy Harris - LITTLE SUITE, p. 3 "Bells",
Copyright 1939 by G. Schirmer, Inc., International Copyright Secured
Used by permission of G. Schirmer, Inc

Ex. 3

Samuel Barber - SONATA, p. 3, l. 4
Copyright 1950 by G. Schirmer, Inc., International Copyright Secured
Used by permission of G. Schirmer, Inc.

Robert Starer - FIVE CAPRICES, p. 3 m. 3-5
Used by permission of Peer International Corporation, New York, Copyright Owners

Juan Orrego Salas - RUSTICA, p. 4 l. 1 m. 4-5, l. 2 m. 1-3
Used by permission of Pan American Union, Washington, D.C.
Sole Representatives: Peer International Corporation, New York

FOR REFERENCE:

Satie - FOURTH NOCTURNE, Esch.
Schoenberg - FIVE PIANO PIECES op. 23, Hansen, p. 5 l. 5 m. 2
Wellesz - FÜNF TANZSTÜCKE, U.E., no. 1
Bartók - OUT DOORS, U.E., "Barcarolla"
Piston - CONCERTINO, Arrow
Bloch - VISIONS AND PROPHECIES, Schr., p. 3 l. 3-4, p. 10 l. 2-3
Sowerby - TOCCATA, Mercury, p. 1 l. 1-4
Liebermann - SONATA, U.E., 1st mvt, 3rd mvt
Paz - THIRD SONATINA, ECIC, p. 7 l. 2-3
Helm - CONCERTO IN G, Schott, p. 16, p. 26, p. 33
Villa-Lobos - GUIA PRATICO, SMPC, p. 7 m. 3-5, p. 16 l. 3 m. 3, l. 4 m. 1-3
Khachaturian - CONCERTO, Leeds, p. 14 l. 3, l. 4 m. 1-2
Scriabin - SONATA NO. 8, Leeds (after Lento: Allegro agitato)
Bacon - MAPLE SUGARING, Schr., 10 pieces
Green - TWELVE INVENTIONS, AME, p. 9 l. 2 m. 3-4, l. 3

VIII B

Chords and Progressions of Seconds and Ninths

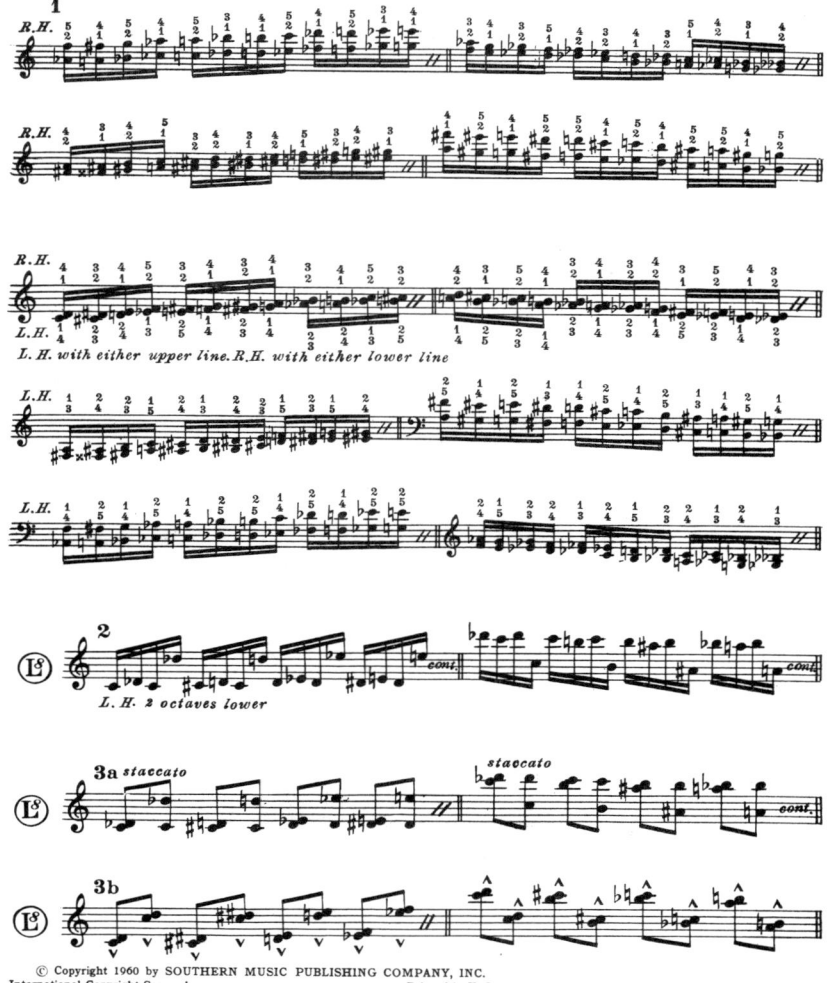

© Copyright 1960 by SOUTHERN MUSIC PUBLISHING COMPANY, INC.
International Copyright Secured   Printed in U. S. A.
All Rights Reserved Including the Right of Public Performance for Profit

28

continue diatonic scales in chromatic progression in both directions

Seconds in the Whole-tone Scales Here in crossrhythm.

Seconds as Ninths. Frequently appearing as Augmented Octaves. Observe Bi-tonality of Two Major Scales in Minor second relation. Can be transposed into any other pair of Major or of Minor Scales.

Ninths symbolyzing Augmented Octaves are applied in a tune as sound effect. The five Black Keys are played either with the thumbs or with the fifth fingers. Any other melody could be treated in this fashion as exercise for this type of setting.

© Copyright 1960 by SOUTHERN MUSIC PUBLISHING COMPANY, INC.
International Copyright Secured   Printed in U. S. A.
All Rights Reserved Including the Right of Public Performance for Profit

Ex. Pesante ($\quarternote = 132$)

Béla Bartók - OUT DOORS, "With Drums and Pipes", p. 5 l. 1
Copyright 1927 by Universal Editions, Renewed 1954
Copyright and Renewal assigned to Boosey & Hawkes Inc. for U.S.A.
Used by permission of Universal Edition (London) Ltd., and Boosey & Hawkes Inc.

Ex. 2

poco a poco cresc.

Béla Bartók - THIRD CONCERTO, p. 46 l. 3, p. 47 l. 1 m. 1-4
Copyright 1947 by Hawkes & Son (London) Ltd.
Used by permission of Boosey & Hawkes Inc.

Ex. 3 Moderato (♩=76)
p espress.   p cristalino
pp   dim.

R. G. Morillo - CONJUROS, p. 9 l. 4-5, p. 10 l. 1
Used by permission of Editorial Cooperativa Interamericana de Compositores, Montevideo
Sole Representatives: Southern Music Publishing Company, Inc., New York

Ex. 4

Luis Gianneo - SONATINA, p. 4 l. 5 m. 4, l. 6 m. 1-3
Used by permission of Editorial Argentina de Musica, Buenos Aires
Sole Representatives: Southern Music Publishing Company, Inc., New York

FOR REFERENCE:

    Ravel - GASPARD DE LA NUIT, Dd, "Scarbo"
    Malipiero - OMAGGI, Chester, "a un papagallo"
    Honegger - CONCERTINO, Senart, 3rd mvt
    Scriabine - VERS LA FLAMME op. 72, p. 5 l. 3-5
    Bartók - OUT DOORS, U.E., "The Chase", p. 29
          MIKROKOSMOS, B&H, Vol. 5, p. 24, p. 25, Vol. 6, p. 16, p. 19
    Villa-Lobos - RUDEPOEMA, Esch., p. 13, p. 14 (Ninths), p. 16, p. 17 (Seconds)
    Toch - CONCERTO NO. 2, Schott, p. 23
    Prokofieff - DEVILISH INSPIRATION op. 4/4
    Bloch - SONATA, Carisch, p. 3 l. 6

VIII c
Tone Clusters

In this Model a famous classical theme (**2nd** movt. of Haydn's Surprise Symphony) is harmonized with Tone Clusters.
Experiment with any other tune in similar fashion.

© Copyright 1960 by SOUTHERN MUSIC PUBLISHING COMPANY, INC.
International Copyright Secured   Printed in U.S.A.
All Rights Reserved Including the Right of Public Performance for Profit

Ex. 1 Moderato scherzando

Henry Cowell - AMIABLE CONVERSATION, l. 2
Copyright 1922 by Breitkopf and Härtel, Inc., New York; Renewed 1950
Used by permission of Associated Music Publishers, Inc., New York

Ex. 2 Lento (♩=72-69)

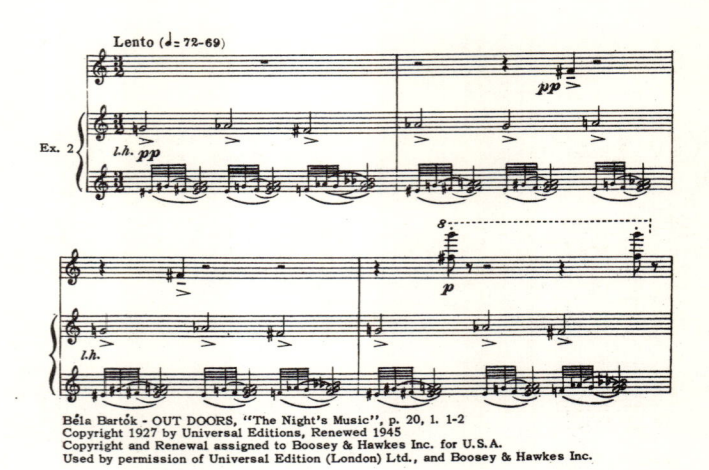

Béla Bartók - OUT DOORS, "The Night's Music", p. 20, l. 1-2
Copyright 1927 by Universal Editions, Renewed 1945
Copyright and Renewal assigned to Boosey & Hawkes Inc. for U.S.A.
Used by permission of Universal Edition (London) Ltd., and Boosey & Hawkes Inc.

Ex. 3 Allegro

Serge Prokofieff - CONCERTO NO. 3, p. 65 l. 2 m. 1-6
Used by permission of Leeds Music Corporation, New York, Copyright Owners

Copyright 1923 Breitkopf and Härtel (A. Gutheil)
Copyright assigned 1947 Boosey & Hawkes Ltd.

Ex. 4 Meno mosso

Meno mosso

Robert Starer - FIVE CAPRICES, No. 4 p. 8 l. 5, l. 6 m. 1-3
Used by permission of Peer International Corporation, New York, Copyright Owners

Ex. 5 Allegro (♩=76-112)

Charles Ives - FIRST SONATA, p. 14 l. 1-2
Used by permission of Peer International Corporation, New York, Copyright Owners

FOR REFERENCE:

Cowell - SILT OF THE REEL and TIGER, AMP
Villa-Lobos - GUIA PRATICO, SMPC, p. 16 l. 1 m. 1-3, l. 2 m. 1
Ives - SONATA NO. 2 (Concord), Arrow, p. 41 l. 5, p. 42 l. 1-2

IX
Polyrythm and crossrhythm

Since such rhythmical inventions cannot conveniently be abstracted in form of Models, quotations have to suffice to present some examples.

Ex. 1

Igor Strawinsky - CONCERTO FOR PIANO AND WIND INSTRUMENTS, p. 52 l. 3 m. 2-4
Copyright 1924 by Edition Russe de Musique; Renewed 1952
Copyright and Renewal assigned to Boosey & Hawkes Ltd.
Used by permission of Boosey & Hawkes Inc.

Ex. 2

Peter Mennin - VARIATIONS-CANZONE (from Five Piano Pieces), p. 8 l. 2 m. 3-5, l. 3-4
Copyright ©1951 by Carl Fischer, Inc., New York
International Copyright Secured
Used by permission of Carl Fischer, Inc..

Ex. 3

Paul Hindemith - LUDUS TONALIS, p. 8 l. 5 m. 1-2
Copyright 1943 by Schott & Co., Ltd.
Used by permission of Associated Music Publishers, Inc., New York

FOR REFERENCE:

Gershwin - RHAPSODY IN BLUE, Harms, p. 18 l. 3-5.
Slonimsky - THESAURUS OF SCALES AND MELODIC PATTERNS, Coleman-Ross
Creston - SIX PRELUDES, Leeds
Tcherepnine - EXPRESSIONS, Leeds, p. 19
Mennin - TOCCATA (from Five Piano Pieces), C.F.
Hanson - CONCERTO, C.F.
Dallapiccola - QUADERNO MUSICALE, Zerboni, No. 4
Dello Joio - THIRD SONATA, C.F., p. 6 Var. 3
Scriabin - VERS LA FLAMME, p. 3 l. 3-5

X
Twelve-tone Music

Ex. 1   The following is an example of a suitable series:

[Ex. 2 — musical notation]

In the twelve-tone technique, only the order of succession of the tones in the twelve-tone series is relevant, regardless of their register. The following series are considered identical with Ex. 2:

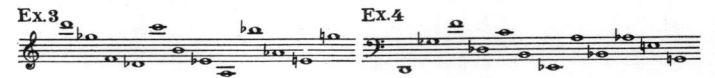

[Ex. 3 and Ex. 4 — musical notation]

Accordingly, in composition, the tones of the series can be used in any octave position, provided only the order of succession remains unchanged.

Ernst Krenek - STUDIES IN COUNTERPOINT, Ch. I p. 1
Copyright 1940 by G. Schirmer, Inc., International Copyright Secured
Used by permission of G. Schirmer, Inc.

Ex. 2   [musical notation]

Arnold Schoenberg - FIVE PIANO PIECES op. 23, p. 16 l. 1 m. 1-4
Copyright 1923 - 1951 by Wilhelm Hansen, Copenhagen
Used by permission of the Publishers

Ex. 3   **PREFACE**

The theme of the "Passacaglia" is built progressively of all the intervals from the minor second to the major seventh.

[musical notation]

The eleven counter-themes are respectively constructed on a 12-tone succession of each of the available intervals.

[musical notation]

Stefan Wolpe - PASSACAGLIA, p. 3
Copyright 1947 by New Music Edition
Used by permission of the Copyright Owner

FOR REFERENCE:

Schoenberg - SUITE op. 25, U.E.
Weber - FIVE BAGATELLES, N.M.
Krenek - SONATA NO. 3, AMP
        EIGHT PIANO PIECES, Mercury
Leibowitz - FOUR PIANO PIECES op. 8, U.E.
Apostel - KUBINIANA op. 13 (Ten Piano Pieces), U.E.
Jelinek - TWELVE-TONE MUSIC op. 15 (in 5 books), U.E.
Riegger - VARIATIONS FOR TWO PIANOS, AMP

INDEX OF COMPOSERS

Apostel, 32
Ardévol, 16
Auric, 17
Bacon, 17, 27
Barber, 10, 26
Bartók, 3, 5, 10, 15, 17, 18, 22, 24, 27, 28, 29, 30
Bloch, 5, 7, 16, 17, 18, 27, 29
Bowles, 10, 18
Casella, 7, 10
Castro, J.M., 17
Castro, W., 17
Chagrin, 17
Chaim, 10
Chavez, 7
Copland, 22, 23
Cowell, 30
Creston, 17, 31
Dallapiccola, 31
Darnton, 18
Debussy, 3, 5, 7, 8, 10, 11, 14, 16, 17, 22
Dello Joio, 18, 31
Egk, 17
von Einem, 14, 18
Feinberg, 17, 20
Fuleihan, 7
Gershwin, 7, 10, 11, 14, 17, 31
Gianneo, 6, 12, 18, 29
Green, 7, 8, 11, 22, 24, 27
Griffes, 5
Halffter, R., 14, 17, 22
Hanson, 7, 23, 31
Harris, 17, 18, 26
Helm, 18, 27
Hindemith, 6, 9, 12, 15, 16, 17, 18, 20, 24, 31
Honegger, 10, 29
Ives, 12, 21, 22, 24, 30
Jelinek, 32
Jolivet, 22, 23
Kabalevsky, 14, 17
Khachaturian, 10, 17, 20, 22, 23, 27
Kodály, 14
Krenek, 22, 23, 26, 32
Kubik, 13, 16, 18, 20
Leibowitz, 32

Leighton, 16
Liebermann, 27
Luening, 18
Malipiero, 29
Martinu, 14
Mennin, 7, 31
Milhaud, 10, 14
Mompou, 17
Morillo, 3, 29
Orrego Salas, 27
Paz, 20, 27
Pisk, 16
Piston, 12, 27
Poulenc, 12
Prokofieff, 5, 7, 8, 10, 12, 16, 17, 18, 20, 22, 24, 29, 30
Ravel, 5, 9, 16, 29
Read, 7, 8
Rebikoff, 3
Reizenstein, 18
Respighi, 7
Riegger, 32
Rorem, 6
Satie, 14, 27
Schoenberg, 20, 22, 23, 24, 27, 32
Schuman, 18
Scott, 5, 8
Scriabin, 20, 22, 27, 29, 31
Shostakovitch, 5, 7, 12, 17, 18, 20, 22, 23, 24
Slonimsky, 10, 20, 24, 31
Sowerby, 27
Starer, 10, 27, 30
Strawinsky, 17, 24, 31
Szymanowski, 18
Tansman, 18, 22
Thomson, 12, 14
Toch, 18, 22, 23, 24, 29
Tscherepnine, 8, 12, 14, 20, 23, 31
Turel, 5
Villa-Lobos, 10, 11, 21, 27, 29, 30
Weber, 32
Wellesz, 18, 27
Wolpe, 32
Wordsworth, 17